TROUT
with
Flair & Taste

by

Jean Malla

Editor: Helen Classon
Food Stylist: Sara Wattie
Photography: Bill Classon
Graphic Design: Dennis Keys

Published and distributed by ☺ Australian Fishing Network
48 Centre Way, South Croydon, Victoria 3136
Telephone: (03) 9761 4044

Australian Bookshop Distributors
Tower Books
Telephone: (02) 9975 5566

USA Importers and Distributors
Frank Amato Publications
PO Box 82112, Portland, Oregon 97282
Telephone: (503) 653 8108

First published 1997
Printed in Melbourne by BB Print Resources
Telephone: (03) 9533 4293

ISBN 0-9587143-3-9

Minister for Inland Fisheries

Foreword

Fishing is one of the most popular pastimes of people of all ages. It has been so for many centuries and will be for many to come.

Tasmania deservedly enjoys its world wide reputation as one of the premier trout fishing locations.

I can remember as a child whiling away many pleasant hours during school holidays, dangling a line in a water where I thought I could catch a fish. I still try to do so.

Like Jean Malla's father, my father was a keen trout fisherman and taught me from an early age the seeking out of the wily trout.

Over my years as a 'hunter gatherer' the role of not only catching the trout, but preparing these magnificent fish, has become mine. Each time I return from a fishing trip with my catch, I search the cookbooks for new and exciting ways to serve my trout. Speaking with other anglers, I hear of, and am sometimes told of special recipes, marinades and smoking methods. But alas! There are only so many ways to cook trout - or are there?

Jean Malla has not only earned a reputation as a skilled trout fisherman with an excellent knowledge of Tasmania's world class wild brown trout, he is also earning a reputation in preparing trout for the table.

On reading Jean's manuscript, I was most impressed with his range of trout dishes, and am looking forward to trying his recipes with great anticipation.

I believe this book will prove to be another worthy lure for all sports people who enjoy catching and eating this magnificent fish - the Tasmanian Trout.

Enjoy trout fishing!

Enjoy preparing and eating your catch!

John Cleary
Minister for Inland Fisheries
Tasmania

* The Hon John Cleary has had Ministerial responsibility for the Inland Fisheries Commission in Tasmania since February 1992.

1

Introduction

My name is Jean Louis Malla. Originally I came from France, where I served my chef apprenticeship at the Nice Hotel School.

My father was a keen fly fisherman and I have followed in his footsteps, actively fly fishing for the past 25 years in various streams, lakes and rivers.

I tie my own flies and have developed some patterns of my own.

Over the years I have caught thousands of trout. To date my largest catch is a 6.5 kg rainbow taken from Lake Sorell in the Central Highlands of Tasmania.

I now live in Tasmania and from my background as a chef I have learned to cook trout in a number of different ways.

I hope the following recipes will help you to cook trout with flair and taste.

In Tasmania, we are very lucky to be able to catch sea run brown trout in the correct season. These fish run all the way to the continental shelf, and come back to feed in the estuaries when the whitebait commence their spawning migration up stream. Sea run trout feed mainly on small fish and crustaceans, including crabs and shrimp and make an excellent table fish.

It is possible to purchase sea run trout which are farmed in the cool waters of Southern Tasmania and these, too, make fine table fish.

Tight lines and appetising trout.

And remember, only take what you need. Our future generations depend upon it.

Jean Louis Malla.

Dedication

To my wife, Rama Malla, who has been so patient with me during my fishing trips and during the time of the writing of the book.

Acknowledgments

I would like to thank my fishing partners, Mr Mark Dewar and Mr Peter Cochrane, who have been so helpful, and I would also like to thank Mr Bill Classon who has given me the opportunity to write this book.

Fishing Cookbook Series 1

Editor: Helen Classon
Food Stylist: Sara Wattie
Photography: Bill Classon
Graphic Design: Dennis Keys

Published and distributed by
Australian Fishing Network
48 Centre Way,
South Croydon, Victoria 3136
Telephone: (03) 9761 4044

Australian Bookshop Distributors
Tower Books
Telephone: (02) 9975 5566

USA Importers and Distributors
Frank Amato Publications
PO Box 82112,
Portland, Oregon 97282
Telephone: (503) 653 8108

First published 1997
Printed in Melbourne by
BB Print Resources
Telephone: (03) 9533 4293

ISBN 0-9587143-3-9

Contents

Filleting

Methods of filleting trout

a) Butterfly fillet

b) Along the bone fillet

c) Without the skin fillet

d) cutlets, or what are known in French as "darne"

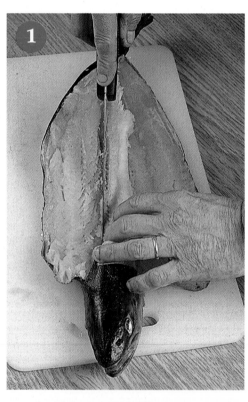

The butterfly fillet

With this method the trout should not be gutted from the bottom of the fish, but filleted from the top. You will need a very sharp filleting knife.

1. Following the back bone you cut along the top of the side of the fish, and repeat the process on the other side. Continue to cut down and off the bone to the belly cavity.
2. When both sides are done cut the back bone near the head of the fish and pull it back towards you. The bone should come away easily with the gut attached.
3. Split the end near the tail and remove the bone and the gut. The fish is now ready to cook.

Hints:

1. *Clean your fish in the water where you catch it.*
2. *Never scale trout.*
3. *Never cut the head off a fish, unless you fillet the fish.*
4. *When you fillet a fish, pull the fish under toward you, if the knife is very sharp the skin will come off easily.*
5. *Always use a sharp knife, a blunt knife can't cut.*

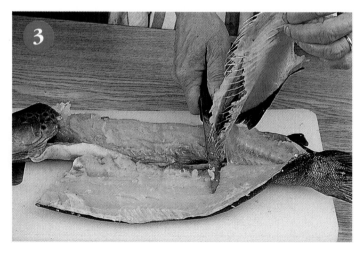

Along the bone fillet

Clean and gut your trout and dry it with a paper towel to stop it sliding out of your hand. Place the dry fish on a board, and make an incision with the knife at the tail. Hold the tail firmly with the aid of a towel and slide the knife along the body until it reaches the head. Repeat the operation on the other side.

Without the skin fillet

Once the trout is filleted (using the "along the bone fillet" technique), dry the fillet with a paper towel. Make a small cut near the tail, hold the skin firmly and pull the fillet towards you - the skin will come off easily.

Cutlets 'darne'

1. Cut the head off the fish near the first fin.
2. Continue to cut the trout across the body; the back bone is very soft and cuts easily.
3. The finished product.

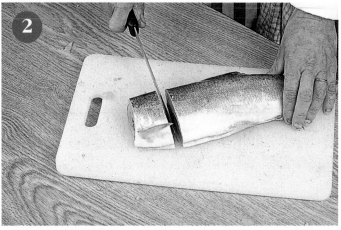

Smoking

More and more people like to eat smoked fish, and trout, in my opinion, are some of the best fish to smoke.

There are actually two ways to smoke trout - cold smoke and hot smoke. The choice depends on the taste of the individual, however both are nice.

Hot smoked trout

My wife bought me a little stainless steel smoker and this does the job perfectly on filleted or whole trout. I find that peppermint wood sawdust is by far the best for this type of smoking. It is quite easy to smoke fish if you follow the instructions when you buy your smoker. I carry mine everywhere, even up to the lake on fishing trips.

Trout with Flair & Taste

Cold smoked trout

Cold smoking is a different kettle of fish. You can buy your own cold smoking mixture in fishing tackle shops, and the method is easy to follow, however I do my own cold smoking. For cold smoking it is important that you use filleted trout only, and it goes like this:

Fillet your fish (using the "along the bone" method), but keep the skin on. Once the fish is filleted, dip the fillets in a salt water mixture (1/2 cup of salt to four litres of water for two fillets - this will help drain off the excess blood): After leaving the fillets in the salt water dip for about half an hour, dry them with a paper towel, then with tweezers pick the remaining bones from the fish.

1. On top of each fillet put some brown sugar and chopped dill.
2. Put the fillets on top of each other, place in a sealed plastic bag, and keep in the fridge for two or three days, turning the bag every night. After the second or third day has elapsed, open the bag and wash the fillets in clean water, then dry them.
3. They are now ready to be eaten or frozen.

Hint: *When hot smoking my trout, I always mix some chopped bay leaves or mixed herbs into the sawdust. Here in Tasmania I used peppermint saw dust, but saw dust is sold in tackle shops all over Australia.*
I also rub some chopped fresh dill on the fillet.

Soups

Trout consomme with dumpling
Consomme de truite aux quenelles

Serves 4 - 6

Ingredients:
1 kg sea trout, filleted and boned out
200 ml dry sherry
3 egg whites
150 g plain flour
salt & pepper to taste
250 g mixed herbs
1 onion
2 carrots
1 stick of celery
4 cloves
1/2 bunch chives
2 litres water

First make the consomme (clear soup). To achieve this place the head and bone from the trout in a deep saucepan, and add 2 litres of water, the onion, carrots, cloves and chopped celery stick. Bring the saucepan to the boil and then cook slowly for about 45 minutes until the soup reduces. Finally, strain it and you are left with the consomme.

To make the dumplings or quenelles:
Cut the trout fillet into big pieces and place them in a food processor. Add the egg whites, flour, herbs and salt and pepper, until you are left with a smooth paste. Form the paste into golf sized balls to form the dumplings.

Into the saucepan containing the consomme, add the dry sherry. Warm the soup on a medium heat and poach the dumplings for a few minutes.

Serve in soup bowls with 3 or 4 dumplings to a bowl, and present with chopped chives.

Picture Top Right: Trout consomme with dumplings

Picture Right: Smoked trout Chowder

Trout with Flair & Taste

Smoked trout chowder

Potage de truite fumee

Serves 4

Ingredients:
1 or 2 fillets of hot smoked
  (or unsmoked, if preferred) trout
  without bone
1 carrot, diced
1 onion, diced
1 stick of celery, diced
chopped parsley
300 ml milk
50 g plain flour
125 g butter
one litre of fish stock
200 ml of medium dry sherry
grated nutmeg
salt and pepper to taste

The first step is to make the white sauce. Melt the butter in a saucepan and add the plain flour, cooking until the mixture is brown (we call this mixture a "Roux"). Then add the milk, stirring slowly so as not to get any lumps, until thickened. When thickened, add the fish stock, stir and let simmer for about 10 minutes. While simmering, in another saucepan fry the diced vegetables in a little butter, and add the trout cut into pieces. Fry for a few minutes, and then add the white sauce mixture from the first saucepan.

Add salt, pepper, and nutmeg to taste. Serve with small pieces of fried bread "croutons."

Warm smoked trout salad
Salade de truite fumee chaude

Serves 4

This recipe is ideal as an entree.

Ingredients:
**2 smoked trout fillets (skinned, and
  without bone)**
1 tablespoon sesame oil
2 tablespoons lime or lemon juice
1 mignonette lettuce
1 punnett of cherry tomatoes
1 tablespoon orange juice
2 tablespoons olive oil
julienne made from the lime or lemon peel
ground black peppercorns
salt and pepper to taste

For the salad: in a stainless steel bowl mix the tomato
and mignonette lettuce with a tablespoon of orange
juice, two tablespoons of olive oil, salt and pepper, and
mix together.

Place the salad mix on the serving dish. Next place the
pieces of smoked trout on top of the salad, add the
sesame oil, the lime or lemon juice, salt, and ground
black peppercorns.

Julienne the lime and serve.

Sashimi trout

Truite a la Japonaise

Serves 4

For this recipe use cold smoked trout. Before you slice the trout, if the fillets are not frozen, place them in the freezer for a couple of hours. If they are frozen, allow them to defrost until the trout is just slightly hard; it is easier to slice the fish when it is near frozen, because it should be cut paper thin.

Slice the filleted trout at an angle, and prepare a side dish of soy sauce. You might like to add some green horseradish to the side dish. Decorate with rice rolled in seaweed and slice. This is delicious served as an entree.

Trout with Flair & Taste

Smoked trout terrine and avocado

Terrine de truite fumee a l'avocat

Serves 4

This terrine is ideal for picnics, the races, a fun day out.

You will need about one kilogram of hot smoked trout fillets to make a decent terrine. Remember to take out all the bones.
Allow the trout to cool.

Ingredients:
**1 kg of smoked trout
1 tablespoon green peppercorns
2 ripe avocados
1 small sachet of gelatin
1 sliced lemon (and some lemon juice)
salt and pepper (optional)**

Place the trout in a food processor and puree until smooth (about one or two minutes), then place in a dish and add the peppercorns.
In the bottom of a terrine mould put as a base some of the dissolved gelatin and lemon slices. Put in the fridge to set.

In the food processor now put the peeled and destoned avocados and the lemon juice, so the avocados won't turn black. Add the leftover gelatin to the smoked trout and mix together.

After the gelatin in the bottom of the terrine mould is set, fill half the terrine mould with half the trout mixture, then the avocado puree and add the other half of the trout mixture on top. Leave to set in the fridge overnight. The next day, take the terrine out of the mould. Slice and serve with thin slices of Melba toast.

Warm smoked trout with garlic mayonnaise

Truite fume chaude a l'ailio

Serves 4

Ingredients:
4 pan size smoked trout
3 egg yolks
2 or 3 garlic cloves (crushed)
1 tablespoon squeezed lemon juice
some very finely chopped chervil
1 tablespoon French mustard
2 or 3 glasses olive oil
salt and pepper to taste (optional)
1 mignonette lettuce

Hot smoke the trout. When smoked, the skin will come off very easily.

The mayonnaise can be made in a food processor, blender etc.
In a bowl put the egg yolks, garlic and the mustard, and mix, adding a little oil at a time. When the mixture has thickened you are ready to add the lemon juice, the chervil, salt and pepper.

To serve, decorate the plate with some mignonette lettuce, and fresh chervil (a spoonful on the side of the plate).

Bon Appetit.

Picture Right: Salsa

Picture Below: Warm smoked trout with garlic mayonnaise

Salsa

Truite fumee

Ingredients:
500 g smoked trout, boned out
250 g sour cream
50 ml lime juice
25 g green peppercorns
25 g chopped coriander
salt to taste

Into a food processor place the smoked trout and all other ingredients, then process for 2 to 3 minutes, or until you get a smooth paste. Serve in a dip dish with corn chips or toast. This is an easy and tasty appetiser.

Entrée & Appetisers

Cold smoked Swedish style trout

Truite Suedoise au gravalat

Serves 4 - 6

Ingredients:
1 kg trout, filleted
1 bunch finely chopped dill
250 g brown sugar
50 ml squeezed lemon juice
25 g black peppercorns
100 ml sour cream
2 mignonette lettuces
200 g cooking salt

Prepare the fillet, making sure all bones are removed: I find that tweezers do the job perfectly.

Soak the trout fillets in water with the cooking salt for about 45 minutes, then wash them meticulously and remove any trace of blood with a paper towel.

Lay the fillets flat, and on top of each fillet put the lemon juice, brown sugar, the chopped dill and the black peppercorns. In an ovenproof bag place the fillets one on top of the other, then seal the bag and place in the fridge for at least 3 days and nights, making sure that the bag is turned every day.

Finally, take the fillets out of the bag and clean and dry them with a paper towel (do not wash them in water). Slice the fillets very finely and serve on individual plates using the mignonette lettuce as a base. Decorate the plates with lemon wedges, a spoon of sour cream, and ground black peppercorns. Also serve with fresh warm toast.

Trout fettucine

Truite aux fettucini

Serves 4

Ingredients:
1 trout of about 1 kilo filletted & skinned
500 g fresh fettucine
500 g white fettucine
50 g pine nuts
200 ml olive oil
2 crushed garlic cloves
100 ml white wine
2 egg yolks
100 ml fresh cream
1/2 bunch basil, finely chopped
200 g freshly grated parmesan cheese
salt and pepper to taste
4 litres water

Mix egg yolk and cream together, beating lightly.

Put 4 litres of water in a pot, add a small amount of olive oil, and bring to boil (the oil will stop the pasta from sticking). Add the fettucine and cook for approximately 8 minutes, until al dente. Strain the pasta and rinse with cold water.

Cut the trout into small finger-like pieces and fry lightly in a large frypan for 5 minutes. Then add the pasta, pine nuts, crushed garlic and wine. Cook slowly for another 5 minutes, stirring from time to time.

Before serving, add the cream and egg yolk mixture to the frypan and stir and let simmer until the mixture thickens.

Serve with a generous amount of chopped basil on top and add the parmesan cheese.

Timbal of trout with seafood

Timbale de truite aux fruits de mer

serves 4

Can be served either as an entree or a main course:
for entrees use 500 g trout
for main courses use a 1 kg trout
The trout must be filleted and boned out.

Ingredients:
1 lemon, squeezed
250 g fresh scallops
250 g cooked king prawns
200 g plain flour
100 g butter
200 ml water
salt and pepper to taste

For the sauce:
150 g tomato puree
150 ml white wine, Burgundy
100 ml double cream or natural yoghurt

Cut the trout into pieces and place in a food processor, add the scallops, king prawns, lemon juice and a touch of salt and pepper. Puree until you get a thick mixture.

To make the choux pastry to be used as a base:
In a medium size saucepan put the water, butter and a pinch of salt, and then boil. Next, take the saucepan off the heat and add the plain flour, mixing the two together using a wooden spoon. Then place saucepan back on the heat and continue to work the mixture with the spoon. Turn the heat down halfway and keep stirring until you are left with a ball that doesn't stick to the side of the saucepan. This is the choux pastry.

Next, butter 4 souffle dishes, place the pastry around the insides of the dishes, then fill the dishes approximately 3/4 full with the seafood mixture, as the mixture will rise during cooking. Then put the souffle dish into a baking dish filled halfway with water and cook in a preheated oven at 180 degrees Celsius (360 F) for about 45 minutes.

When cooked, turn the souffle dishes onto individual plates.

In a heated frypan place the wine and tomato puree, reduce for a few minutes, and add the cream or yoghurt. Serve the sauce on top or around the timbale and decorate with fresh dill or coriander.

Sea trout Tahitian style
Truite de mer Tahitienne

Serves 4

Ingredients:
1 kg sea trout, filleted and boned out
1 tin coconut milk
2 finely chopped lemons
1 spring onion, finely chopped
50 ml lemon juice or lime juice
1 coarse lettuce
4 empty coconut shells (fo serving)
salt to taste

Cut the fillets into cubes and place in a bowl, then add the rest of the ingredients and leave in the fridge to marinate overnight.

Put one or two lettuce leaves in each of the coconut shells and then add the fish mixture.

Cold and delicious, ideal for summer.

Main Courses

Sea trout with prawns & Bearnaise sauce

Darne de truite de mer aux crevettes & Bearnaise sauce

Serves 4

Ingredients:
2 kg sea run trout cut into cutlets
250 g cooked or uncooked
   king prawns
3 egg yolks
250 g butter
200 ml of white vinegar
small amount of tarragon
   (fresh or dry)
a few black peppercorns

It is possible to buy the Bearnaise sauce, but I prefer to make my own. A lot of people say it is hard to make, however if you follow this recipe it will not curdle.

Pour into a saucepan the vinegar, peppercorns, and tarragon. Bring to the boil and then simmer on reduced heat until a small amount is left. Strain.

Place this strained liquid and the egg yolk in a stainless steel bowl. Beat the mixture on top of the stove over a moderate heat until fluffy. Melt the butter and slowly add to the fluffy egg mixture, beating slowly until mixture thickens. You now have your Bearnaise sauce.

Fry the prawns in a little butter or olive oil, and when cooked place in a bowl. Next, pan fry the trout approx. 5 minutes each side. When cooked place onto a serving plate. Put the prawns on top of each cutlet and cover with the Bearnaise sauce. Place under the grill for a few minutes and serve.

Grilled trout thyme

Truite grille au thym

Serves 4

This is a recipe for people who watch their cholesterol - it is very simple and cholesterol free.

Ingredients:
2 kg sea trout cut into 4 cutlets
100 ml olive oil
1 sprig Lemon thyme
2 limes or lemons squeezed

Brush the olive oil on both sides of the fish cutlets and place under grill at medium heat. Cook both sides for approx. 5 minutes each side, depending how thick the fish cutlets are. Add a small amount of pepper to taste.

In a small saucepan, add the left over olive oil, a squeeze of lime or lemon juice and thyme and gently heat. Pour over the fish and serve with a mesclum salad (ideal for this dish) with a salad dressing of olive oil and lemon or lime juice.

Picture Above: Left Dish - Sea trout with prawns & Bearnaise sauce
Right Dish - Grilled trout thyme

Sea Trout with fennel

Darne de truite de mer au fensuil

Serves 4

Ingredients:
4 sea trout cutlets
50 ml Pernod
2 fennel bulbs, lightly blanched in
  boiling water
small bunch of coriander
pepper & salt to taste
200 ml cream

In a frying pan add olive oil and small amount of butter. Cook the trout cutlets for 5 minutes each side, and when cooked flambe with the Pernod, then remove from stove. Cut the fennel in julienne. In another frypan melt a little butter and fry the fennel for a few minutes. With the frypan that contains the fish add some cream and chopped coriander and let it reduce.

Put the fennel onto a plate as a base and place the fish cutlets on top, then pour sauce over dish.

WARNING: Do Not Flambe with Fan On or Range Hood operating.

Trout with Flair & Taste

Trout with freshwater yabbies

Truite aux ecrevisses

Serves 4

Ingredients:
1 kg lake trout filleted and cut into 4 serves
1/2 glass of brandy
250 g yabbies cleaned and shelled
150 ml tomato puree
150 ml sour cream
50 ml olive oil and 50 g butter
salt and pepper to taste

In a frypan melt the butter and add the olive oil. This combination stops the butter burning. When hot cook the trout fillets for 5 minutes each side. When cooked place fillets on a serving plate. Add the yabbies to the frypan together with the remaining ingredients. Cook slowly for a few minutes and then put the yabbies on top of the trout. Let the sauce reduce and then pour over dish.

One day a friend of mine, Kerry, and I decided to go and see if there were any sea trout about. It was a nice, windless October morning and the tide was nearly high, when walking along a dirt road that runs alongside the Derwent River I spotted some weed and decided to wade waist deep toward it. It was very calm and some whitebait were working along the edge of the weed. Unfortunately for me the tide was too high and I landed in water too deep too quickly! A fish was starting to chase the whitebait along the edge of the weeds. Frustrated, I was unable to reach it.

Kerry and I decided to return home, fishless. On the way back Kerry spotted a little hole on the side of the road and decided to cast into it. His fly landed in a little hollow. Bang! He hooked a 3 and 1/2 pound sea trout. How lucky can you get?

On returning home I used the trout to make the next recipe (Trout Veronica) for Kerry and myself - it was delicious!

How to get your trout...

Trout are available commercially everywhere in Australia, from Queensland right across to Western Australia. So if you aren't an angler, don't worry. Farm trout are available in butcher shops, supermarkets and seafood shops. Fantastic Tasmanian sea run trout and Atlantic salmon are also available now and represent some of the best fish in the world!

Personally I prefer to catch my own, but don't forget catch and release. I only take what I need for my family, the rest go back to swim for another day. Our future generations depend on us, how we manage our fisheries.

Trout Veronica

Truite Veronique

Serves 4

Ingredients:
4 pan sized whole trout, or
  1 kg lake trout filleted into 4 serves
1 glass of white wine (preferably Moselle)
1/2 cup white grapes
1 cup cream
chopped dill
oil and butter
salt and white pepper

In a frypan pour the butter and oil. Flour the trout both sides and when oil is hot cook both sides of the trout on medium heat. To the same frypan add the white wine, grapes, cream, and salt and pepper to taste. Reduce the liquid for a few minutes and serve. Spread the chopped dill on top of the dish and serve with sliced cream potatoes and fresh vegetables.

Provencal trout
Truite a la provencale

Serves 4

Ingredients:
4 pan sized whole trout, or
  1 kg lake trout cut into 4 serves
200 ml wine, dry Riesling
150 ml tomato puree
2 crushed garlic cloves
chopped parsley
very finely chopped shallots
50 g black olives without seeds, cut in half
150 ml pure olive oil
salt and pepper to taste

In a frypan pour the olive oil. Lightly flour the trout both sides and when the oil is hot cook the trout on a medium heat for approximately 10 minutes each side. When the trout is cooked select a low heat setting and add the white wine, black olives, tomato puree, garlic, shallots, chopped parsley, salt and pepper. Cook for another 5 minutes and then serve. Garnish the plate with a green salad, small new potatoes and fresh vegetables.

Trout meuniere
Truite Meuniere

Serves 4

Ingredients:
4 pan sized whole trout, or
  1 kg lake trout
filleted into 4 serves
150 ml wine, dry Riesling
chopped parsley
1 tablespoon butter
small glass lemon juice
salt & ground black pepper to taste

In a frypan melt the butter and add a dash of oil. Lightly dip the trout in plain flour. When oil and butter are hot cook each side of the trout for approximately 5 minutes until the skin is crispy. When the trout is cooked add the wine, chopped parsley, lemon juice and salt and pepper and let the mixture reduce.

To serve the trout, pour over the sauce and garnish with thin lemon slices and a lemon wedge. Garnish the plate with parsley and serve with a mesclum salad and thin (pomme allumette) French fries.

Picture Left:
Left Dish - Provencal trout
Right Dish - Trout meuniere

Main Courses

Fillet trout Nice style
Truite farcies a la Nicoise

Serves 4

Ingredients:
4 pan sized whole trout,
  cleaned and gutted
250 g lean minced beef (topside)
1 small finely chopped onion
2 small cloves of garlic,
  finely chopped
sprig fresh thyme
1 egg white
2 tablespoons virgin olive oil
150 ml white wine (optional)
black pepper and salt
For the sauce -
pinch sweet basil
small glass dry white wine
small glass tomato puree

Firstly marinate the beef. In a bowl put the minced beef, egg white, onion, chopped garlic, black pepper and salt, fresh thyme and white wine. Mix all the ingredients together well and leave in the fridge for 24 hours.

Now fill each trout with the marinated mixture. Pour some olive oil into a pan and heat. When hot put trout into pan and turn over. Place in oven pan and bake in a moderate oven for about 15 to 20 minutes. When cooked place trout on serving plates and make up a sauce. Use chopped basil with a little dry white wine and some tomato puree. Reduce and pour over the fish.

Serve with side dishes of fettucine verde, garnish with fresh basil.

Monte Carlo trout
Truite a la Monte Carlo

Serves 4

Ingredients:
4 pan sized whole trout
150 ml white wine
100 g fresh or frozen scallops
250 g peeled king prawns
250 g chopped spring onions
150 ml fish stock if possible.
Otherwise poach the scallops and
  use the stock.
100 ml cream
grated nutmeg
1 cup olive oil
salt and pepper to taste

Fill each trout with some cleaned scallops and prawns. In a frypan, pour the olive oil, white wine and stock together. Warm pan on a medium heat and add the trout, then cover pan and simmer for approximately 10 minutes. When cooked place the trout on individual serving plates.

Now add to the pan the cream, salt and pepper, spring onions and nutmeg. Reduce and pour a small amount of sauce on each fish.

Serve with small new potatoes and pan fried snow peas.

Picture Right:
Top Left Dish - Fillet trout Nice style
Bottom Right Dish - Monte Carlo trout

Trout with almond sauce

Truite almondine

Serves 4

Ingredients:
4 pan sized whole trout (approx. 250 gr
  each) or 1 kg lake trout cut into 4 serves
1 glass of white wine, Chablis if possible
20 grams of slivered blanched almonds
1 glass of cream
white pepper and salt
50 gr butter
50 gr olive oil

In a frypan place melted butter and a dash of oil. When hot, lightly flour the trout and cook both sides for about 5 minutes until the skin becomes crispy. Place the trout on a serving dish. Add the wine to deglaze the pan then add the almonds and the cream. Reduce for a few minutes and pour over the fish. Serve with souffle potatoes and fresh crispy vegetables. Garnish with celery leaves.

Poached trout in mango sauce

Truite poche aux mangues

Serves 4

This recipe is for those who like their food to be low in cholesterol.

Ingredients:
4 pan sized whole trout or
　1 kg lake trout filleted and cut into 4 serves
1 carrot sliced
1 celery stick sliced
1 small onion, pickled with 2 or 3 cloves
1 bouquet garnish (thyme and rosemary)
1/2 lemon cut into 2 wedges
150 ml white wine, Burgundy if possible
100 g natural yoghurt
100 g sliced mango

Put the fish into a pan and add all ingredients except the yoghurt and mangoes. Cover and cook for about 10 minutes. Place the fish on a plate and let the remaining juice reduce. Add half a cup of natural yoghurt and pour over the fish. Serve with steamed potatoes and steamed vegetables. Puree a tin of mangoes and serve a couple of tablespoons on the side of each plate.

Back in early April, 1996, I was fishing at Arthurs Lake in a bay known as Transmission Line Bay, which is part of a large area of water named the Cow Paddock. When the lake level is high this bay is ideal for trout fishing. Transmission Line Bay is a beautiful little area, protected by the prevalent north-westerly and south-westerly winds, and is fairly weedy, so the wading is very good.

On one particular trip to this area I left the boat at home and chose to wade in waist deep water, using a floating line and two small flies. After a couple of hours fishing I had received no strikes, let alone seen any sign of a fish. Another couple of fly fisherman were also fishing near me in the bay, and I became friends with one of them. His name was Peter Sylvester, and I do quite a lot of fishing with Peter to this day. I don't recall the other fisherman's name. Peter had also been fishing with a floating line, and seeing he had had very little luck also I decided it was time to change tactics.

While Peter and his friend continued to fish without any luck I returned to the car and changed to a sinking line, also changing my fly to a size 8 hook on the tippet with a size 10 dropper. I returned to the water and after just 15 minutes, bang! I landed a beautiful 2 kilo brown trout in excellent condition. soon after I landed another one and a half kilo brownie, and two more about a kilo in weight, which I returned to the water. From nothing I had ended up with four beautiful fish, all due to a change in line. Peter and his friend who continued to use the floating line caught nothing!

As a result of this day I learned the importance of carrying different line and changing tackle often.

These days there is quite a lot of controversy about how much cholesterol people should have in their bodies. These recipes will be suitable for people who are health conscious - it is just a matter of using close substitutes for some of the ingredients eg. replace the cream by a natural yoghurt which has a low fat content.

The wine included in some of the recipes is added to give a little more flavour to the dishes. Most alcohol in the wine has been evaporated by the time the dish is cooked.

I do hope you find these recipes new, exciting and refreshing. In my opinion trout is one of the best table fish if it is cooked with flair and taste.

Bon appetit.

Poached trout madrilene

Truite poche madrilene

Serves 4

A low cholesterol recipe.

Ingredients:
4 pan sized whole trout (250 g each) or
  1 kg lake trout filleted and cut into 4 serves
Coarse lettuce leaves
Half a glass of dry white wine
Salt and pepper to taste

Wrap the fish individually in coarse lettuce, after adding salt and crushed black peppercorn to taste. Fill the pan halfway with a mixture of 1/2 a glass of dry white wine and water. Cover and cook the fish for about 10 minutes. Place the fish on a plate and pour over the remaining juice. If desired add a squeeze of lemon juice and serve with a mixed green salad together with olive oil and lemon dressing.

Curry trout

Truite a l'indienne

Serves 4

Ingredients:
1 kg trout cut into 4 cutlets
1 large onion finely chopped
3 or 4 garlic cloves crushed
crushed ginger
1 tablespoon squeezed lemon
1 teaspoon curry powder (masala)
2 tomatoes diced
1 teaspoon of Marsala
1/4 teaspoon tumeric
small amount of mustard seeds and
cumin seeds andred chile, if desired
1/4 cup of oil
salt and pepper to taste

In a saucepan heat oil, and add the garlic, ginger, onion, mustard seed and cumin seed. When lightly brown add the tomatoes and chile, tumeric and Marsala and reduce heat. When the ingredients begin to stick, put the fish in and gently stir together, taking care not to break the fish. Add salt and pepper to taste together with enough water to just cover the fish. Let simmer on a moderate stove for 10 to 15 minutes. When mixture thickens add lemon juice and serve with steamed long grain rice.

Picture Left:
Top Left Dish - Poached trout madrilene
Bottom Right Dish - Curry trout

Main Courses

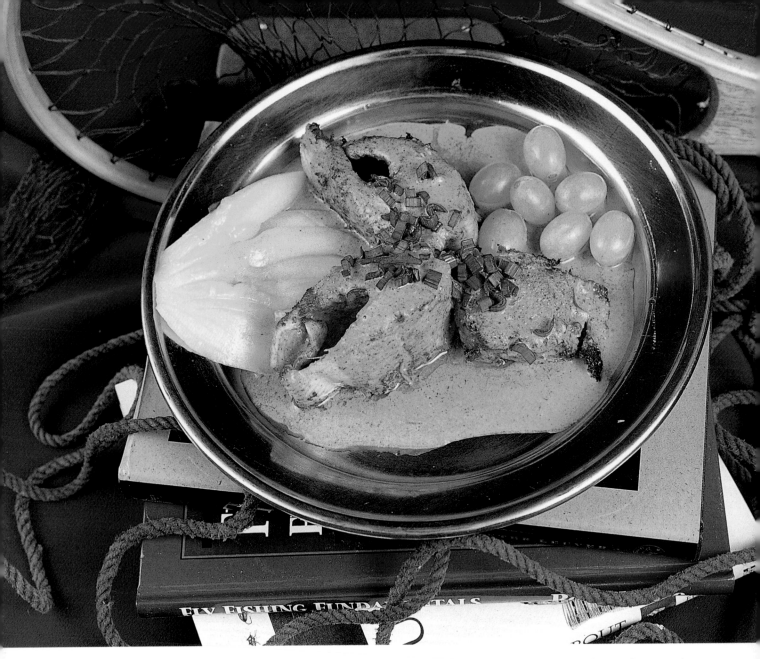

Fried trout Madras

Truite Madras

Serves 4

Ingredients:
4 cutlets from a large lake trout
1 egg
1 cup plain flour
1 teaspoon Masala (curry powder)
1/4 teaspoon tumeric
1/4 cup lemon/lime juice
2 crushed cloves of garlic
chopped red chile (if desired)
salt and pepper to taste

In a bowl mix the egg (lightly beaten), Marsala, tumeric, lemon/lime juice, salt and pepper, garlic and chile together until it becomes a smooth paste. Marinate the fish cutlets in the paste for 15 to 20 minutes. Dip in plain flour and fry in hot oil for 5 minutes each side until crispy.

Serve with fried rice cooked in tumeric, with fresh chopped coriander.

Trout with wild mushrooms

Truite Duxelles

Serves 4

Ingredients:
4 whole pan sized trout, approximately
  250 g each
500 g wild mushrooms
150 ml dry white wine
1 bunch spring onions
2 whole eggs
25 g mixed herbs
150 ml olive oil
50 g butter
2 lemons
salt and pepper to taste

First, to make the duxelles, which is a puree of wild mushrooms, put the mushrooms, spring onions, eggs and salt and pepper in a food processor and puree for about 3 to 4 minutes until you are left with a paste.

Next, fill each individual trout with the paste, place them in an oven dish and then cover them with the wine. Add the herbs, lemon juice, oil and butter. Cover with foil and bake in an oven at 200 degrees C (400 F) for 20 minutes.

When serving the trout pour the excess juice over the fish for sauce. Serve with vegetables or a crispy salad and a tangy French dressing.

There is a bay in Arthurs Lake in the Central Highlands of Tasmania called Seven Pound Bay - I always wondered why the bay had been given this name.

One day I met a nice old gentleman on one of my fishing trips. His name was John Phillips and after talking to him for a while I discovered he was the founder of the fly tiers club in Hobart. John told me that the bay received its name because years ago he himself caught a seven pound brown trout from there, and so appropriately named the area Seven Pound Bay.

It is amazing who you can meet when you go fishing.

In Lake Sorell, Tasmania, in the 1900s there was a guest house on the southern shore of the lake, and personalities from those days used to come to the lake and fish. One day I went to visit the guest house, which is now falling to ruin, and I was looking through the guest book when I saw the signature of Charlie Chaplin with the comments "Thank you for the trout dinner," so I set out to find what they served him. Fortunately, the recipe was in the book.

In those days there were no fridges, so they used to clean, gill, and hang the fish in a fish safe. After the trout had been hanging in the fish safe for a couple of days all the blood dried off, and with the sun and the wind, it became like smoked trout.

We still use fish safes today, when we go fishing for a few days.

The Charlie Chaplin trout recipe

Serves 4

Ingredients:
1 whole 2 kg trout
250 g wild mushrooms (when available -
  otherwise the humble white mushroom
  will suffice!)
1 glass of Riesling white wine
1 cup double cream
1 squeezed lemon
salt and black peppercorns crushed to taste
butter or oil

Cook the trout on a barbecue or open fire when the coals are red, for about 10 minutes on each side.

In a saucepan melt the butter and fry the mushrooms for a few minutes, then add the white wine, and let it reduce. Next add the cream, reduce again, and finally add salt and pepper to taste. Add the lemon juice at this point and the sauce will not curdle. The lemon juice adds a tangy taste to the sauce.

Serve the trout on a plate, and pour over the sauce. "Voila trout Chaplin".

Steamed trout mandarin

Truite poache mandarin

Serves 4

Ingredients:
2 kg trout, filleted and cut into four serves
1/2 glass rice wine
1 tablespoon sesame oil
1/2 cup soy sauce
2 tablespoons lime juice
sprinkle of chopped coriander
julienne of carrots and celery
2 small choy cabbages
1 glass fish stock

For this recipe you will need a wok and a bamboo steamer.

In the bottom of the wok pour the fish stock and sesame oil. Put the steamer in the wok, and then the fish in the steamer. Steam for about 10 minutes.

For the sauce, while the fish is cooking, in a bowl mix together the rice wine, soy sauce, lime juice, and coriander. Add the julienne of vegetables on the top of each fillet of fish.

When cooked, dish up each fillet on a separate plate, pouring the sauce over each fish. Serve with small choy cabbage and decorate the fish with fresh coriander.

Trout with Flair & Taste

Trout Andalousian

Trout a l'andalouse

Serves 4

Ingredients:
4 whole trout approx 250 g each
1 red capsicum
1 green capsicum
150 ml Spanish olive oil
4 or 5 cloves of crushed garlic
5 g thyme
5 g rosemary
10 g ground black peppercorns
150 ml dry white wine
10 g finely chopped parsley
salt to taste

Finely chop the thyme and rosemary and then mix together.

Capsicum has been known to give upset stomachs to some people. To help avoid this put the capsicum under a grill and roll occasionally until the skin on the whole capsicum is burned. If using gas this can be achieved by placing the capsicum in the flame and repeating the same process. When the skin is burned peel it off whilst running the capsicum under cold water, remove the seed and then cut the capsicum into long strips. Place the strips in a bowl and add 50 ml olive oil, and the garlic and herbs, which will act as a marinade.

In a large frypan put the rest of the olive oil, then lightly flour each fish and add to the frypan when the oil is hot. Cook the fish for approx 5 minutes each side or until the skin is nice and crispy. Remove the trout and in the same frypan place the capsicum, wine, and the rest of the ingredients and cook for a few minutes until the wine reduces.

Pour the mixture over the top of the fish, add the chopped parsley, and serve with garlic bread and green garden salad, with fresh orange juice and olive oil dressing.

Trout in the mud

Ingredients:
2 kg trout
1 lemon cut into wedges
salt and pepper
some good mud
a good campfire

Clean and gut the trout, and fill the inside with lemon wedges. Wrap the fish in mud or clay, and when the fire has died down a little and the red hot coals are left, dig the trout wrapped in the mud in the hot coals and cover the top with the rest of the coals. Cook for 45 minutes and "Bob's your uncle."

Serve with a nice hot damper.

Baked trout in alfoil

Truite en papillotte

Serves 4

Ingredients:
2 kg trout, whole cleaned and gutted
2 tomatoes, sliced
1 lemon, sliced
1 large onion, sliced into rings
50 ml white wine (optional)
sprinkle of mixed herbs
salt and pepper to taste
100 ml olive oil
1 piece of alfoil

1. First catch your trout and waht a beauty this one is!
2. Put a piece of alfoil in the bottom of a tray, making sure you have enough to wrap around the whole trout. On top of the trout put one slice of tomato, lemon, onion, and repeat the procedure until the end of the fish is reached. Then add the salt and pepper, mixed herbs, olive oil and the wine.

Wrap the fish and bake in a moderate oven for about 30-35 minutes, or until the fish is cooked.

Serve on a large plate, and fillet while serving.

Pictures 1, 2 & 3: Baked trout in alfoil

Tasmania - it's a place full of history from the old convict days, but I did not realise this until I started to do some research for this book, and found a few amazing stories about what the older generation called "the good old days".

I am talking about the late 1800s, which in my opinion were not "good old days" at all!

Anyway, one story goes that an ex-convict came to the Central Highlands of Tasmania (after being pardoned), and built a house in the bush; he even built a road, which is now flooded by Lake Sorell. The ex-convict got married and had a child (a boy I was told). Shortly after, he committed another crime (namely murder); and the British soldiers came after him.

Knowing he would face certain death if caught the ex-convict left his wife and boy and went to California, America in the gold rush and became a millionaire!

The following recipe comes from the old days, and can be cooked today as well, when you are away camping. I call it trout in the mud!

This last recipe comes with a little story.

I was fishing Lake Sorell one day with one of my friends, when he suddenly screamed, "I've got one!" "Oh, good, trout for dinner tonight," I replied.

After 15 minutes of battle, the fish hadn't been sighted. With rod bending, I said "It's a big rainbow, I think." After a little while longer it came into view. Oh my, a tiger snake! The shock was too much for him so I cut the line. Oh well, we could have had a snake dinner!

Something to talk about around the campfire, "the tiger snake which got away, not the Tasmanian tiger after all."

Trout the easy way

Butterfly the trout as shown previously, add some butter or margarine, sprinkle salt and pepper, a small drop of beer on the fish. Place the butterfly fillet (meat facing the fire) on a green forked branch and cook on an open fire for a few minutes. Serve with a nice hot damper.

This is the easy way to cook trout

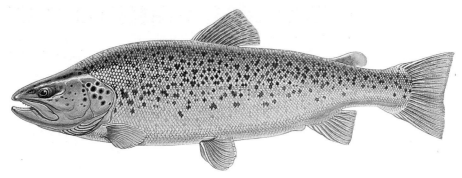

Merlin Cunliffe
Fish Painter

Merlin Cunliffe lives in the Yarra Valley in Victoria with his wife who is a botanical artist. He has exhibited at a number of galleries in the Yarra Valley and Melbourne and had joint exhibitions with his wife in Adelaide.

Merlin currently has his most recent artwork on display at Australian Fishing Network, 48 Centre Way, South Croydon, Victoria.

He studied painting and calligraphy with the botanical artist Wilfrid Blunt at Eton College in England but had started painting fish at the age of 5 when living in America. He worked as a graphic and product designer in the 1970s and 1980s and has more recently owned and ran a fish farm in the Yarra Valley.

Merlin has produced a series of limited edition prints of goldfish and was commissioned to produce a print of a Tasmanian Brown Trout for the 1988 World Fly Fishing Championships. He was subsequently commissioned by Mr Jim Allen of the Compleat Flyfisher to produce a pair of limited edition prints of a rainbow and a brown trout.

He has produced many pen and ink and watercolour illustrations for aquarium fish magazines and written many articles on the subject of gold fish varieties. In 1982 he produced a number of illustrations of game fish for an Australian fishing magazine.

Merlin has been commissioned to produce paintings for a former Prime Minister of Australia and a former Prime Minister of Canada.

What's on at the NATIONAL FISHING CENTRE

NATIONAL ANGLERS GALLERY

ON SHOW

Original Watercolours by Merlin Cunliffe

All Enquiries - Annette (03) 9761 4044

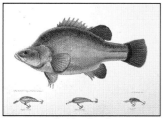

Golden Perch
Gold Framed Original $890

Brown Trout
Gold Framed Original $650
Also Gold Framed Print $39.95

Mangrove Jack
Gold Framed Original $860

Murray Cod
Gold Framed Original $1040

Bream
Gold Framed Original $570

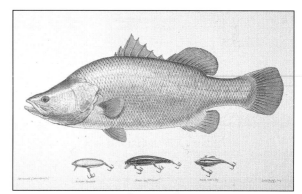

Barramundi
Gold Framed Original $990

COME AND VISIT - OPEN TO THE PUBLIC

National Fishing Centre
Headquarters of the

AFN
AUSTRALIAN FISHING NETWORK

Freshwater Fishing MAGAZINE

Australian and New Zealand
Flyfishers Annual

Geoff Wilsons Knots & Rigs

NATIONAL FISHING CENTRE
48 Centre Way, Croydon South, Victoria
Tel: (03) 9761 4044
Open: 9-5.30pm, Mon-Fri. Melway Ref: 51 B9